The Boy and the Bears

A Native American Pawnee Tale

retold by Elizabeth Smith
illustrated by Jim Gordon

Harcourt
SCHOOL PUBLISHERS

Requests for permission to make copies of any part of the work should be addressed to School Permissions and Copyrights, Harcourt, Inc., 6277 Sea Harbor Drive, Orlando, Florida 32887-6777. Fax: 407-345-2418.

HARCOURT and the Harcourt Logo are trademarks of Harcourt, Inc., registered in the United States of America and/or other jurisdictions.

Printed in China

ISBN 10: 0-15-350494-3
ISBN 13: 978-0-15-350494-5

Ordering Options
ISBN 10: 0-15-350333-5 (Grade 3 Below-Level Collection)
ISBN 13: 978-0-15-350333-7 (Grade 3 Below-Level Collection)
ISBN 10: 0-15-357481-X (package of 5)
ISBN 13: 978-0-15-357481-8 (package of 5)

2 3 4 5 6 7 8 9 10 985 12 11 10 09 08 07

Cast of Characters

Storyteller

Chief

Little Bear

Bear Cub

Cub's Mother

Cub's Father

Scene One

Setting: *The Chief is walking through a forest. On the ground is a bear cub, crying.*

Storyteller: One day, a Pawnee chief was walking home. He glanced down, and he saw a bear cub. It was crying for its mother. The chief gently picked it up to console it.

Chief: Little one, are you lost? Are you hungry? (*He pulls food out of his bag and gives it to the Cub, who eats it quickly.*) You like that, don't you? I think you are becoming drowsy. (*He places the Cub on the ground. Then he covers it with leaves.*)

5

Chief (*To Cub.*)**:** You are safe here until your mother comes. You know, my wife and I are expecting a baby. If my child is ever alone, I hope there will be someone to help, just as I have helped you. Sleep well. Your mother will be here by the time you wake up.

Storyteller: The Chief walked on until he reached his village. He told his wife about the bear cub. When their son was born, they named him Little Bear after the bear cub. As Little Bear grew, he did many heroic things. He was always helping others.

Scene Two

Setting: *Outside a cave where bears live. Little Bear, a young man now, is sitting and thinking. The Chief walks up to him.*

Chief: You have been sitting here for hours, Little Bear. Why?

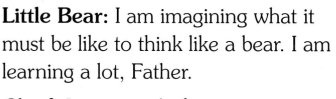

Little Bear: I am imagining what it must be like to think like a bear. I am learning a lot, Father.

Chief: I am proud of you, my son.

Scene Three

Storyteller: One day, Little Bear was running in the forest. Then he hurt his leg. He lay on the forest floor for a long time. Soon two bears came along. (*Little Bear lies very still on the forest floor.*)

Cub's Mother (*Pointing at Little Bear.*)**:** Look! That is the young man who sits outside our cave. He looks like he is hurt. Please help him.

Cub's Father (*Picking leaves and pressing them on Little Bear's leg.*)**:** Let's take him back to our cave. (*They all exit.*)

Scene Four

Setting: *A hilltop.*

Storyteller: Little Bear stayed in the cave with the bears for weeks. He got better. He also learned more and more about the bears. One day, the father bear walked him to the top of a hill. They stood together for a moment.

Cub's Father: You have learned much. Go back to your people now. May you go on to be a great chief. (*Exits.*)

Little Bear (*Calling after Cub's Father.*)**:** Thank you, my friend.

Storyteller: Chief Little Bear became known as a wise leader. He was known for helping his people, not scolding them. Every year, he held a ceremony to honor the day the bears had saved him. He taught his children and grandchildren all he knew. To this day, the Pawnee understand the power of the bear. They also know it is not a burden to help someone in need.

Think Critically

1. How does the Pawnee Chief help the little bear cub?

2. What is the theme of the play?

3. How is what happens in Scene One like what happens in Scene Three? How is it different?

4. Why is the play divided into scenes?

5. If you were acting in this play, which character would you want to be? Why?

 **Drama**

Write a Missing Part Write another scene for this play. Have the mother bear find her young cub in the forest. He is covered with leaves the way the chief left him. What would the mother say? What would the cub say?

School-Home Connection Act out this play with family members. Take turns playing the different roles in the play.

Word Count: 522